Railway Walks
from
Stratford
by John Roberts

© John Roberts 2006
ISBN 0 947708 44 8

WALKWAYS

**John Roberts 67 Cliffe Way, Warwick
CV34 5JG 01926 776363**

john@walkwaysquercus.co.uk
www.walkwaysquercus.co.uk

The Countryside Code
respect – protect - enjoy

Be safe – plan ahead and follow any signs

Leave gates and property as you find them

Protect plants and animals, and take your litter home

Keep dogs under close control

Consider other people

Updating Service

The countryside changes all the time. Paths are diverted and hedges removed, there are new tracks, fences and barns. To keep walk directions up to date I issue Updating Slips - a unique and **free** service.

Phone or Email me (number and address on the back of the title page) with a note of the books that you have and I will send you up to date Slips. **Even new** or recently purchased books can suffer changes within weeks.

Please write, phone or email to report any changes or problems, stating book title, walk and paragraph number.

Don't bother copying changes into your book(s). Just dab affected paras with highlighter and keep the Slip in the front pocket of the plastic cover provided with it.

Chapel Gate
(Henley to Danzey)

Stratford Canal near
Wootton Wawen

The Walks

	miles	kms
Stratford on Avon to Wilmcote	3	5
Wilmcote to Wootton Wawen	5.5	9
Wootton Wawen to Henley in Arden	3.7	6
Henley in Arden to Danzey	3.7	6
Danzey to Wood End	2.5	4
Wood End to The Lakes	2.25	3.5
The Lakes to Earlswood	1.25	2
Earlswood to Wythall	1.5	2.5
Wythall to Shirley	3	5
	-----	----
	26.4	43

IMPORTANT: Sunday trains do not stop at Wootton Wawen, Danzey, Wood End or Earlswood.

Hedges, Woods and Hills

The stations on the Birmingham - Stratford on Avon line are all attractive. Many of them have kept their Great Western Railway character, or had it restored, with the red brick buildings, traditional name boards, fretted platform canopies, neat footbridges and cream and ochre paintwork.

The stations are also quite close together, and once you are out of the urban areas the line runs through the green and hilly Warwickshire countryside. These walks on field paths and farm tracks link all the stations between Stratford and Shirley, except for Whitlock's End where there are only road connections.

The walks are described from south to north (Stratford to Shirley) with clear, step by step directions, and there are notes about pubs, cafes, buses and car parks. Start from one station, walk to the next and catch a train back. The longest walk is only 5.5 miles/9 kms so people with old, young or tired legs can probably manage one. The more active can take in two, three or the whole lot, a distance of 26.5 miles/43 kms.

North from Stratford the land rises slowly to Wilmcote, fields of crops giving way to grassland. After a few miles of green and level fields the walk drops sharply through woodland into the valley of the River Alne. You follow its winding way through water meadows fringed with willows and alders to Henley.

North from Henley there are small hills in a more intimate landscape of thick, winding hedges with sturdy old trees and patches of woodland. This continues through Danzey and the pretty village of Tanworth in Arden to Wood Green.

Walking on to Earlswood Lakes there are the same patterns of trees and hedges but the land is more level until it falls towards the reservoirs. The short walk on to Earlswood station is one of the best, with its views over the water and woodland.

The walk to Wythall is in two level stretches sandwiching a long descent to cross the young River Cole, then a long and rising hedged track. The last walk to Shirley rises and falls gently as it skirts the urban edge of Solihull but stays rural to near its end.

The Shakespeare Express

On summer Sundays since 1999 steam trains have run twice daily from Snow Hill station in Birmingham to Stratford on Avon and back. They are hauled by historic steam engines from Tyseley Locomotive Works, a part of Birmingham Railway Museum which specialises in repairing and restoring steam engines.

The Museum's collection includes three of the GWR's 4-6-0 Castle class engines which were used on fast, mainline passenger expresses, *Clun Castle, Defiant* and *Earl of Mount Edgecumbe.* A regular visitor has been *King Edward I.* Then there is one of the smaller 4-6-0s, *Rood Aston Hall,* a stray LMS Jubilee class engine, *Leander,* and three of those happy little Great Western 0-6-0s with squared pannier tanks.

The two trains each way between July and September make a steamy, nostalgic contribution to the scenery. They will not be of much practical use if you are following these walks because between Birmingham and Stratford they stop only at Tyseley, but you could join them on another day. For details of times and fares phone 0121 708 4960 or turn up www.vintagetrains.co.uk which includes email access. And if you really like this sort of thing you could visit the Museum at 670 Warwick, Road, Tyseley, Birmingham B11 2HL.

Walking the Walks

First, get a timetable for the line. The general pattern has not changed much in recent years. For Autumn 2005 the arrangements were:

Weekdays and Saturdays - trains between Shirley and Stratford ran hourly with an extra service between 17.00 and 18.00 hrs. Last trains left Shirley at 20.48. The Lakes, Wood End, Danzey and Wootton Wawen were request stops. To get on signal to the driver. To get off ask the conductor to stop at your station.

Sundays – services were again hourly with last trains at 18.38 from Shirley. The Lakes was a request stop but trains **DID NOT STOP** at Earlswood, Wood End, Danzey or Wooton Wawen, Notes about this appear in the walks affected.

Distances in yards or miles are to give you a rough idea how far to walk. You don't need to measure because there will be something to look out for, such as a T junction or a brook. **Distances in paces** are to be counted.

Half R/L means a half turn, or about 45 degrees. **Bear R/L** means a narrower angle than a half turn, or just tending away from straight ahead. A **road** is tarmac with a white line down the middle. **Lanes** are tarmac but smaller and with no white line. **Drives** are the same as lanes but not public. **Tracks** are wide enough for four wheeled vehicles and might have an earth, grass or stone surface, but not tarmac. A **path** may have any surface, from mud to tarmac, but is only pedestrian width.

You will get along fine so long as the directions seem to make sense. If suddenly, they don't, go back to the last point at which they did and think again. If you are still confused most probably something has changed, and if you can't work it out go back to the start.

The maps are sketches to a rough scale of 2.5ins/1 mile or 4cms/1km. If you want Ordnance Survey maps to help you find starting points and for general interest get Explorer maps at 1:25,000, 2.5 inches = 1 miles/4 cms = 1 km. You would need numbers 220 – Birmingham and 205 – Stratford upon Avon.

Stratford upon Avon to Wilmcote

Length: 3 miles or 5 kms.

Getting there: Hourly trains. Buses come from all directions. You can use the station car park but it costs £2.50 per day.

Refreshments: Stratford has more pubs, cafes, tea shops and restaurants than I can count. At Wilmcote there are two pubs, the Mary Arden and the Masons' Arms, and a café at the Visitor Centre.

The Walk: The short urban walk as you leave Stratford will take only 10 minutes before you reach the canal, and from there the way is entirely rural. It runs to Wilmcote in a near straight line but the canal's gentle curves and gradual rise through 12 locks give constant changes of scene.

The **Stratford on Avon Canal** starts 26 miles away at Kings Norton in Birmingham where it branches off the Worcester and Birmingham Canal. Fifty-five locks bring it down to the River Avon and on this walk you pass 12 of them. The Stratford was started in 1793 in the early days of modern civil engineering and it meanders through meadows and around little hills to avoid changes of level demanding large cuttings, tunnels and embankments. The promoters ran out of money several times and it took 23 years to complete. Look out for the little split iron bridges designed to let towing ropes pass through without detaching the horse.

Stratford station breathes a gentle nostalgia, with its traditional Great Western Railway colours, buildings and furniture. It is all set off by the enormous laurel bushes behind the island platform and the lone Corsican pine at the bridge.

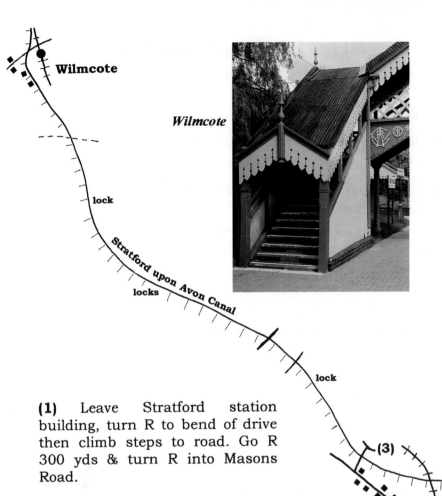

Wilmcote

Wilmcote

lock

Stratford upon Avon Canal

locks

lock

(3)

(1) Leave Stratford station building, turn R to bend of drive then climb steps to road. Go R 300 yds & turn R into Masons Road.

(2) Go 550 yds then turn R up Timothy's Bridge Road. Cross bridge then turn immediately R to join canal.

Stratford upon Avon

(3) Pass under bridge, follow canal 2.5 miles to flat road bridge with green railings & take path up to road. Wilmcote station is 100 yds R.

Wilmcote to Wootton Wawen

Length: 5.5 miles or 9 kms.

Getting there: Hourly trains. Buses call. There is no station car park so park carefully in the street. Walkers must not use the car park of the Mary Arden House.

Trains: CAUTION – trains do not stop at Wootton Wawen on Sundays.

Refreshments: In Wilmcote there are two pubs, The Mary Arden and the Mason's Arms. Mary Arden's house and the adjacent Shakespeare County Museum have a café. At Aston Cantlow you will find the King's Head and at Wootten Wawen The Bull's Head.

The Walk: This is the longest walk between any two stations on the Birmingham – Stratford line, but very easy going. The only feature that might slow you down in wet weather is a short section approaching Aston Cantlow, which can be muddy. The first couple of miles are through a level, undramatic landscape made pleasant by hedgerows, trees and clumps of woodland. The sharp, steep drop through woodland near Aston is quite unexpected and marks a change of scene as you enter the valley of the River Alne and follow it all the way to Wootton Wawen.

Wilmcote station dreams amongst the fields, a small country trainstop from the age of steam. The original steel footbridge has the GWR name cast into the supports and the canopy sports cheerfully oversized finials. The red brick buildings are in English bond; note the fine joints and chamfered corners.

Mary Arden's House and Shakespeare Country Museum. For centuries people believed that Shakespeare's mother had lived at Palmer's Farm. Built in 1569, timber framed and picturesque, it was the perfect setting. Then in 2000 it was discovered her home until she married John Shakespeare in

heading for
Aston Cantlow

waterway
tradition

1557 had been next door at Glebe Farm, a more modest and ordinary red brick building built in about 1515. It was a working farm until 1968 when it was bought by the Shakespeare Birthplace Trust.

The domestic interiors are typical of country living until quite recent times. In the old farm buildings there is a fine yellow wagon with red wheels, wheelwrights' and blacksmiths' shops and a large collection of tack for riding and hauling carts. Worth a visit on their own are the traditional breeds of farm animals such as Longhorn cattle, Cotswold sheep and Gloucester Old Spot pigs, which have been supplanted by breeds that grow fatter, faster or woollier.

The **River Alne** makes its first appearance on this walk but you will meet it again near Danzey and at Tanworth in Arden. From a scurrying brook between low hills it has become a fair sized river cutting a winding but determined channel through a flat, willowy landscape. At Alcester the Alne joins the River Arrow and heads for the Avon.

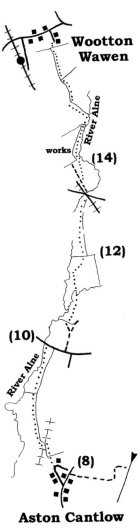

(1) From station go to road & turn L. Go 500 yds to T junction.

(2) Go R 100 yds to opposite Post Office & take drive R. Follow grass track then fenced path & cross two stiles into corner of paddock.

(3) Follow R hedge to field corner & cross stile. Go on a few paces & cross 2nd stile into field.

(4) Follow L hedge/fence 800 yds to stile L. **Don't cross it**. Carry on by hedge & pass projecting hedge corner [*perhaps divert via gateway in new wire fence*] to cross corner stile.

(5) Go ahead parallel with L hedge & cross stile. Follow L hedge to next field corner & cross hidden plank & stile.

(6) Go on by L hedge to cross 2nd plank & stile. Follow fenced path across small field & cross stile onto track.

(7) Go L 200 yds up to double steel gates & turn R on rough track. Go 1 mile/1.8 kms to road at Aston Cantlow.

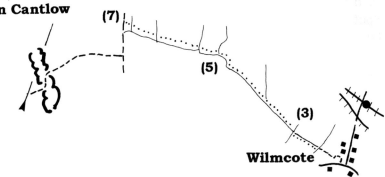

(8) Go L 100 yds & turn R (*Chapel Lane*). Go to sharp R bend but keep ahead on stone track & cross stile. Follow L fence & cross stile L, then 2nd stile.

(9) Turn R past projecting hedge corner, walk with hedge/fence on your R & cross stile. Go on by R fence till it bends R, then bear L to gate & cross stile onto lane.

(10) Don't cross here, go R up grass verge for 200 yds then cross & take track. Go 150 yds then fork L on grass track & cross stile.

(11) Follow path through trees to cross bridge & stile. Go ahead but bear L towards tree clump to cross wide ditch, then bear R & take gate in mid-fence.

(12) Follow R fence/hedge curving R & head for blue brick bridge. Cross stile & follow track to lane.

(13) Go L across river to gateway. Take small path L of concrete track for 100 yds & cross stile onto track. *[If path overgrown use track.]* Face up track then bear R to R end of steel mesh fence.

(14) Follow river, take small gate & cross stile into field. Go ahead by field edge, pass 1st stile R & go on 300 yds to cross 2nd stile R.

(15) Go L by fence 300 yds to cross next stile. Follow L hedge/fence to houses & cross stile.

(16) Follow footway to road & go L to T junction.

[17] Wootton station is 300 yds L. If walking on to **Henley** turn R to A3400 & start the walk at paragraph 2.

River Alne

Wootton Wawen to Henley in Arden

Length: 3.7 miles or 6 kms

Getting there: Hourly trains. Buses call. There is no station car park so park carefully in the street.

Trains: CAUTION – Sunday trains don't stop at Wootton Wawen.

Refreshments: At Wootton Wawen there is the Bull's Head and there are lots of pubs·and cafes in Henley.

The Walk: This easy stroll hardly varies in level as it follows the Stratford Canal and the River Alne. Both roll slowly through a landscape of willows and alders, though the wooded track linking them is lined with field maple.

Wootton Wawen and its church have an immensely long and complicated history. Britons from perhaps 2000 BC, Romans, Saxons and Normans all made their contributions. This is the only Warwickshire church with any Saxon stonework and it dates from about 850 AD. As with all old churches, St Peter's has been repaired, enlarged and altered in just about every later century and displays a mixture of architectural styles. It is built of the local blue lias stone and Arden sandstone but both types decay quite rapidly and have needed endless repair work and constant fund raising. The gargoyles are hideously worn. Go and see, get the booklet which is easily the best of its type I have seen, and leave a lot of money to help keep it all going.

Wootton Hall is a large, square mansion built in the same local lias and sandstone as the church. From a distance the design may seem chastely classical, but the vast and portentous pediment over a fairly modest front door and the enormous, carved coat of arms are very much in the theatrical, decorative baroque spirit.

Puck's Dyke is the name given to the complex of ditches and banks which you cross as you leave the village. It lies close to an ancient ford across the River Alne but no one seems to know its purpose.

The **cast iron aqueduct** carries the Stratford on Avon Canal over the A34, which was once the main road between Birmingham and Stratford. Beyond it is Wootton Wawen Basin with its hire boat yard. Basins along this canal were built at the points it had reached on the several occasions between 1793 and 1816 when work stopped for lack of cash.

(1) From Wootton station take path to road & turn R. Go 400 yds to A3400.

(2) Go R 200 yds to just past shops & take drive R. Take gate then stile ahead. Follow R wall then line of hawthorns along rough causeway to cross footbridge.

Wootton Hall

split bridge on the Stratford Canal

St Peter's Wootton Wawen

ALTERNATIVE: *The Right of Way runs half R through a gate and the field beyond may be very muddy. If so you may take this reasonable alternative.*

(3) IF field is too muddy:
Turn half L past projecting hedge corner to meet drive by gateway. Follow R fence/hedge & cross stile, follow path through trees to lane. Go R 100 yds & turn L up track to canal. **Next –para (5).**

(4) IF field is passable:
Go half R & take small gate, then keep same line & take 2nd. Follow L fence through 2 gates to lane. Go L 75 yds & turn R up track to canal.

(5) Go L 1 mile/.6 km to Bridge 51 & turn L down track to lane.

(6) Don't cross here, go R 200 yds (over bridge) to "Beware" sign, then cross lane & take small steel gate.

(7) Cross field diagonally & take corner stile. Follow riverside track for 500 yds until it enters another field.

(8) Head for red house & go 100 yds to end of R hedge. Bear L to tin roofed shed, & exit to drive.

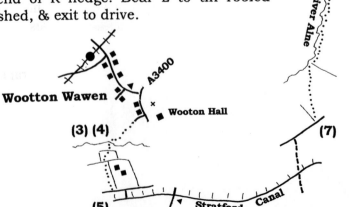

14

(9) Pass house on your R but at its far corner turn R to cross small bridge. Follow fenced path to sports field.

(10) Bear R to where far end of wooden fence meets far hedge, & take small gate onto A3400.

(11) Go R to traffic lights & turn L (New Rd). Go 50 yds & take tarmac drive R. Go to its end & follow path to road.

(12) Go L to fork then R past post box to T junction. Cross road & go R 100 yds to Henley station.

Henley in Arden to Danzey

Length: 3.7 mile or 6 kms.

Getting there: Hourly trains. Buses call. There is a station car park.

Trains: CAUTION – Danzey Green is a request halt and trains don't stop there at all on Sundays.

Refreshments: There are plenty of pubs and cafes in Henley but none at all on the walk.

The Walk: At just under 4 miles this is one of the longer walks on the line and perhaps the prettiest. There is not a single ploughed field but a green and rolling golf course, a modest rural church, a deep, dark wood and gentle hills and dales with fine views.

Henley in Arden station still has the sleepy air of a quiet, rural stop. The steel footbridge and platform canopy have been modernised but with a couple of convincing looking wooden seats and the Great Western Railway colours they convey a strong impression of the past.

The **Arden Way** is a 26 mile circular tour of the woods and green hills of Arden country and you will see its logo on the first part of this walk. Starting from Henley, it visits the villages of Ullenhall, Studley, Spernall, Coughton, Alcester, Haselor, Great Alne and Aston Cantlow; a scenic one day outing for the fit or shorter steps for the rest. Get details by sending £1.65 to Jeanette Norman, 99 Alcester Road, Hollywood, Birmingham B47 5NR 0121 430 7064.

Mockley Wood lies down the flank of a steep hill. From the footpath you can see oak and lime, chestnut, holly, hazel, yew, sycamore and birch with a few Norway spruce and larch. There are clumps of spiky regrowth from coppice stools but much of this part of the woodland seems to be unplanned, self seeded and rather neglected.

(1) From village side of station, cross line by footbridge & turn immediately R. Follow fenced path 120 yds & take steps down to lane. (*Bear Lane*).

(2) Climb steps opposite & cross stile. Follow railside path 600 yds to grass bank. Turn L to join stone path, then drive.

(3) Follow drive between carpark entrances & up to row of conifers. Go R on track 100 yds to fork.

(4) Go R with hedge on your L, pass pool on your R & go on by hedge to cross stile. Go L by hedge to gate & cross stile. Go R, pass barn on your R & take gate onto lane.

(5) Go L round R bend to end of white house, turn L & take gate/stile. Follow green track 200 yds up to (not through) small gate. Go R & cross stile into field.

(6) Go L by hedge & follow past two gateways plus 250 yds, then turn L through gap onto lane. Go R 175 yds to gateway L & take steel kissing gate.

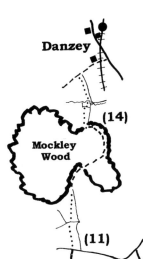

Danzey

Mockley Wood

(14)

(11)

(9)

(7)

Chapel Gate

(5)

(3)

Henley in Arden

(7) Go ahead by L hedge & take kissing gate. Follow L hedge into churchyard. Exit through double gates, go ahead 50 yds to fence & take kissing gate R.

(8) Follow wooden fence R round corner to next corner. Go ahead down line of oaks to bottom hedge & take kissing gate onto junction of lanes.

(9) Go ahead 40 yds & take kissing gate L. Follow R hedge & take 2nd. Go ahead to twin oaks & take 3rd, keep ahead & take 4th kissing gate to junction of lanes.

(10) Go ahead (Gentleman's Lane) 400 yds to lane L, & cross stile R.

(11) Go ahead to field corner gateway & cross stile. Turn half R, follow R hedge to field corner & cross stile.

(12) Go ahead on fenced green track to wooden seat. Go on with fence on your L to corner of wood, & cross stile.

(13) Follow path down through wood for 450 yds & take gate into field.

(14) Go ahead parallel with R fence & cross stile into fenced area. Cross footbridge, go up with fence on your R & take kissing gate onto hard track.

(15) Pass farm & cross railway to road. Go L 225 yds to Danzey station.

Danzey to Wood End

Length: 2.5 miles or 4 kms

Getting there: Hourly trains. No buses. There is a station car park.

Trains: CAUTION – Both Danzey and Wood End are request halts and trains don't stop at either on Sundays.

Refreshments: The Bell, Tanworth in Arden, The Old Royal Oak at Wood End

The Walk: A stroll though green fields with thick hedges in a well wooded landscape visiting the beautiful village of Tanworth in Arden. You cross the infant River Alne twice and the railway four times.

Danzey Station has no reason to exist except Tanworth in Arden and you have to wonder how it would have drawn much traffic even when the line was built in 1908. It has the row of Corsican pines found at so many GWR stations, some original fencing and traditional nameboards, but the concrete shelters and footbridge are not lovely.

The **River Alne** rises at Pink Green to the south-west of Tanworth, flows all around the village then heads south-east for Henley in Arden. At Alcester it joins the River Arrow which in turn joins the Avon. This walk crosses the Alne twice, first by

from
Tanworth in Arden
churchyard

Danzey with
Corsican pines

Chapel Gate

the footbridges near the start and later after the village where you cross the railway. Winding between the fields, fast and clean, the Alne is Grade B on the Environment Agency's quality scale and has brown trout as far downstream as Little Alne.

In **Tanworth in Arden** houses of all heights and shapes jumble happily along the main street. Some of the fronts are colour washed but this is a typical Midlands village of red brick. Most of the buildings are Victorian with a few from the late 18th century. There is a wine shop, a pub with post office, a general store and a school. Do visit the large and fine church, get the leaflet which tells you all about it and leave piles of cash.

(1) From Danzey station exit onto road. Don't cross. Go R 200 yds to gate R.

(2) Take gap L of gate & cross stile. Go L by hedge, follow its bends to gate & cross stile. Go R by hedge to pass under railway & into field.

(3) Go half L & cross footbridge. Turn L to cross 2nd bridge. Go ahead by embankment 300 yds, take gate/stile L & pass under railway.

(4) Take gate/stile (may be bust). Go ahead to cross footbridge. Follow L hedge around field corner & up to projecting hedge corner, then cross stile L.

(5) Follow L hedge to next field corner & cross stile. Follow fenced path to lane.

(6) Go R 25 yds & take steps & kissing gate L. Go ahead, pass the holly tree on your R & follow R fence to enter churchyard. Go ahead, pass church on your R & exit at Tanworth in Arden.

(7) Go R to The Bell. Go L 350 yds to pass "Bellfield" R, then on 50 yds to drive of "Little Court".

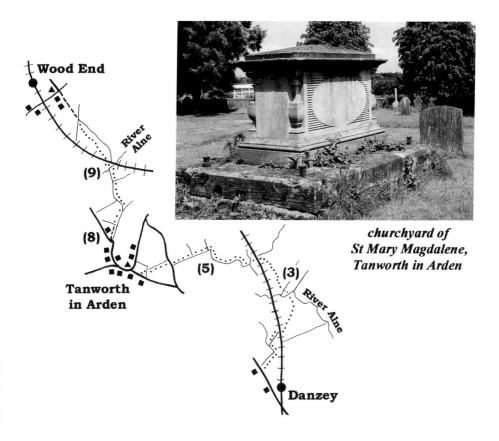

churchyard of
St Mary Magdalene,
Tanworth in Arden

(8) Turn R into fenced path & cross stile into field. Follow R hedge & cross stile. Go L down hedge (via gate & stile) to bottom field corner, to cross stile & bridge.

(9) Go ahead to meet railway fence & follow it L to gate. ***GREAT CARE – LOOK & LISTEN.*** Cross stile & rails into field. Turn L, head for top R field corner & cross stile. Follow wooded track to B4101.

(10) Wood End Station is 100 yds L. If walking on to **The Lakes** take the lane opposite, then turn to paragraph **(1)** at "...follow the lane.".

Wood End to The Lakes

Length: 3 miles or 5 kms.

Transport: Hourly trains. Buses call irregularly. There is no station car park; use the layby on the bridge or nearby street parking.

Trains: CAUTION – Wood End and The Lakes are request halts. Trains do not stop at Wood End on Sundays.

Refreshments: The Old Royal Oak at Wood End.

The Walk: A stroll through level grassland bordered by hedges and trees.

Wood End station is sunk deep in a woody cutting next to the only tunnel on the line. It has its original GWR name boards but the concrete shelters and footbridge are quite charmless.

The **North Worcestershire Path** is a 27 mile walk which runs from Kinver Edge in the west to Shirley, so you will meet it on the walk to Shirley station. Less well known is the **Midland Link**, a 20 mile addition which runs from the NWP via Clowes Wood, Earlswood Lakes and Tanworth in Arden to Kenilworth Castle. You can tell you are on it from the little oak leaf logos on the footpath arrows. This is a well wooded landscape of small hills and small rivers with fine churches and many interesting buildings. If you enjoy this railway walk you will certainly enjoy the Link, a brilliant creation. And I ought to know because I wrote it. (North Worcs. Path & Midland Link - Walkways £5.95).

(1) From station get onto road & go L to pub. Turn L & follow lane .5 mile (past white house R) to white garage L, then turn L & cross stile.

(2) Go R & cross stile under oak tree. Go ahead & cross 2nd stile. Go L by hedge & cross stile onto lane.

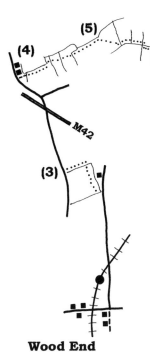

The Lakes

(3) Go R .5 mile (over M42 & past lane R) to 25 yds before 1st house R, then take path R.

(4) Cross stile & follow L hedge to field corner. Bear L to cross bridge & stile. Go ahead & cross bridge, then follow L hedge to where it turns away L at isolated stile.

(5) Go half R to field corner & cross stile. Follow R hedge to cross 2nd stile, then turn R & cross 3rd. Go L by hedge to field corner & cross stile. Go R 6 paces then turn L to houses & cross stile.

Wood End

(6) Go ahead through iron gates & follow track between buildings to lane. Go L to station.

The Lakes to Earlswood

Length: 1.25 miles or 2 kms.

Transport: Hourly trains. Buses call infrequently. There is no station car park so park carefully in the main road or the one opposite.

Trains: CAUTION - The Lakes is a request stop.

Refreshments: none at all; sorry.

The Walk: This very short walk is one of the best for interest and quality. There are the lakes, clean, blue and edged with trees. You can walk right around them but note that some of the paths might be muddy. The woods are confusingly crossed and recrossed by wide tracks between well grown trees and between them is a maze of secret paths through the undergrowth. You will not be here long but it should be long enough to persuade you to come back

Earlswood Lakes were built in the 18th century to feed the Stratford on Avon Canal. A long and high dam was built across the valley where several streams joined to form the River Blythe. The river runs on from an outlet under the centre of the dam while the canal supply flows out in a channel on the northern corner. The lakes are beautifully wooded with groups of shrubby trees forming little islands and inlets. Don't miss a stroll across the leafy causeway which divides two of the pools.

Clowes Wood and New Fallings Coppice cover 115 acres that you can explore as you wish. Varying levels of soil acidity and boggy areas with shallow pools create different types of habitat. There is oak and birch woodland, patches of beech, alder and willow in the wet places with areas of bilberry, heather, carpets of bluebells and lily of the valley. This walk takes you through the Coppice while Clowes Wood is on the other side of the railway.

Earlswood

(1) From station get onto road & turn L. Go 100 yds then turn L down Clowes Wood Lane & walk to its end. Take small gate, follow fenced path to its end & take small steel gate R.

(2) Cross bridge & go L to cross 2nd bridge. Turn L over 3rd bridge, then follow path 33 paces to fork.

(3) Go R & follow wide track up wood edge to within sight of black timber hut. Curve L to fork, go R to 25 paces from hut, then turn half L & cross footbridge into field.

(4) Go L along wood edge & cross stile by car park. Turn L, pass two L forks & go downhill to cross bridge.

(5) Ignore paths R & L but bear R up main track to clearing & stop by three trunked oak. Turn half R to join small path along wood edge & cross stile L into field.

(6) Bear R to end of projecting trees, then join wooded track to stile & road.

(7) Earlswood station is 200 yds L. If walking on to **Wythall** don't cross road, go R 250 yds to opposite double gates, then cross road & enter field. Turn to next walk paragraph 2.

Earlswood to Wythall

Length: 1.5 miles or 2.5 kms.

Transport: Hourly trains. No buses. Use the small station car park but if it is full do not inconvenience nearby residents.

Refreshments: none at all; sorry.

The Walk: For a walk which follows three ruler straight lines this one is surprisingly attractive, skirting some fields, crossing the little River Cole then following a long, wooded path beside a golf course. Even the final road section is pleasant.

The **River Cole** rises in the green and hilly land to the north of Redditch then flows north-east via Shirley to Birmingham. You can follow it on footpaths through the suburbs until it emerges into countryside again near Coleshill. This walk crosses the young, clean river meandering between tree roots where it is graded B or better on the Environment Agency's scale. In the suburbs the water looks more murky but stays mainly at grade C until it joins the River Blythe at Coleshill and drops to E.

(1) From station get onto road. **Don't cross here**. Go R 400 yds to double steel gates L near white house, then cross road & enter field.

(2) Follow R field edge 200 yds to end of trees, then turn R to cross recessed stile. Cross 2nd stile & follow L hedge 400 yds crossing 3rd & 4th stiles.

(3) Turn half R to gate & cross stile. Pass under railway & cross bridge. Follow L hedge 75 yds then cross plank bridge L. Follow rising, hedged track to road.

(4) Cross road & go R .4 mile to station.

(5) IF walking on to **Shirley** then 150 yds short of station turn L into Littleshaw Lane. Turn to next walk & start from paragraph 1, sentence 2.

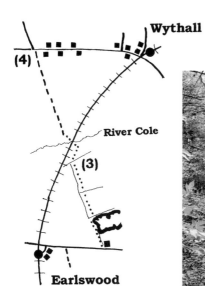

Wythall

(4)

River Cole

(3)

Earlswood

*hedged track
near Wythall*

Wythall to Shirley

Length: 3 miles or 5 kms.

Transport: Hourly trains. Buses are infrequent. There is no station car park so park carefully in nearby streets.

Refreshments: The Draw Bridge pub is towards the end.

The Walk: A beautiful green track leads you to a road and onto the North Worcestershire Path. There is some tarmac but most of the walk runs through fields of riding school horses. The last section crosses the abandoned Shirley Quarry where trees and shrubs are recolonising the pits and mounds.

Wythall station has just concrete shelters and, strangely, no seats, but it still has a remnant of its past in the attractive wooden ticket office, and there is greenery all around.

Berry Mound is a few yards off route where a great ring of trees marks the double ramparts enclosing a 4.5 hectare Iron Age fort. It stands on fairly level ground and does not seem to be the sort of place that the old military engineers would usually choose, but it is surrounded on three sides by the River Cole.

Shirley station has survived pretty well since GWR days. The original brick buildings with their fretted canopies are still in use with the long, wooden benches, and all painted in the old colours. Only the footbridge is modern.

(1) Leave station & turn R. Pass 1st first road R & go on to take next (Littleshaw Lane). Walk to its end then continue on tarmac path to road.

(2) Take fenced path opposite (becomes hedged track) for 350 yds, to gate, stile & road.

(3) Cross road to footway & go R 650 yds to crossroads. Go ahead 150 yds & cross stile L.

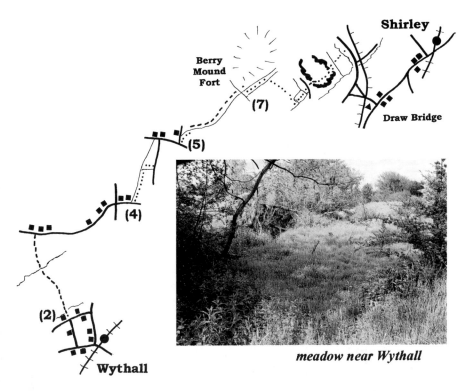

meadow near Wythall

(4) Walk up hedge & cross corner stile. Go R & cross stile onto drive. Go L up to road. Cross to footway, go R 175 yds to gateway & cross stile into field.

(5) Go L & round end of sheds to cross stile. Follow woodchip (later paved) track 100 yds, then turn L & cross stile to reach stone track.

(6) Go R, pass gateway R & cross stile. Follow track 300 yds to its end at gate. Go ahead 12 paces & cross stile R.

(7) Go L on wide fenced track 200 yds & cross stile R. Face downhill, head 30 yds R of white house to gate, & cross stile.

(8) Go ahead by R fence & cross stile onto drive. Go ahead on concrete track then bear R & pass concrete apron on your R to path fork.

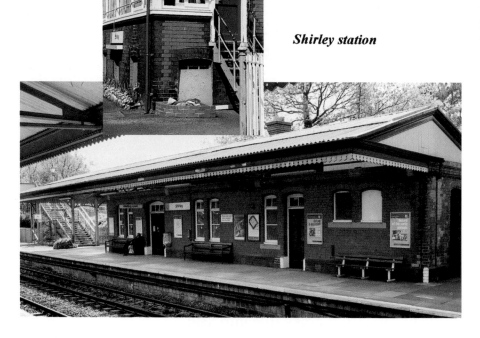

Shirley station

(9) Fork L & follow path to cross stile. Go ahead & cross next stile. Keep same line to cross bridge, then continue to stile & road.

(10) Cross road & go R to junction. **GREAT CARE - LOOK R & L**. Cross road, take footbridge & follow path, then walk on L side of road to next junction.

(11) Traffic has to slow down for bridge, but TAKE CARE. Go L up R side of road to junction & cross drawbridge. Go ahead to main road & turn L. Go 500 yds & cross railway to Shirley station.